# Experience, Opinions & Observations

A COLLECTION OF POETRY

by
Dorette "Doty" Chapman

Follow on Social Media

@PoetDorette/poetdorette

Instagram
Twitter
TikTok
YouTube
Snapchat

Facebook Fan Page
DotyThePoet

To purchase additional copies of this book or poetry-related merchandise, please visit www.dotythepoet.com



ISBN 978-1-7354807-0-1

Please send inquiries to:
BrownSilk Media LLC
PO Box 6731
Lancaster, CA 93539

I dedicate this book to my children,

Dorette, Dorell and Tejre,

who have always been supportive of my efforts, even during the difficult times. Thank you for hanging in there.

## Something To Say

I'd like to thank you for supporting my literary efforts. I am so excited to share my poetry publicly for the first time. Although I've been writing poetry since I was a young child, I have finally arrived at a stage in my life where I am willing to share these thoughts openly. Writing has been very therapeutic for me and allows me to express myself in ways I didn't realize I could. It has also allowed me to share my happiness, fears, heartbreak, humor, imperfections and strengths.

My fascination with how people interact with one another has incited poetry that surveys various stages of life and relationships, many states of emotion, and how dynamic life can be. No matter where I am in life, I know that I must always remember that this journey is carnal and spiritual; and that as long as I am alive, one cannot exist without the other.

My hope is that what I've shared in this text is motivational, uplifting, inspirational, thought-provoking and/or therapeutic for the reader. Please feel free to share your feedback.
Sincerely,

Dorette "Doty" Chapman

# Table Of Contents

# REFLECTION

The journey isn't always great, but almost always worth it!

## Cycle: Life Of Bliss

Childhood can be beautiful
because innocence is bliss.
You're content with all you have
and have nothing to miss.
Your existence thrives through family.
Your environment's your home.
You can explore everything
and you're free to roam.
You're taught how to treat others
and you're taught self-care
and if you need a little help,
your family's always there.
As you get a little older,
your responsibilities grow.
You learned about survival skills
and other things you need to know.
The time then comes to take flight.
You're no longer boys and girls.
You are men and women now
who are ready for the world
You were validated all your life
and met with all your needs.
You pursued your goals and conquered them.
You were destined to succeed.

## Cycle: Life Of Haze

Childhood can be tragic
and lead to a life of haze.
When exposed to turmoil early on,
your perception grays.
When you're too young to care for self
and your needs aren't met,
you are afraid because you've learned
there is no safety net.
When you are lacking nurturing,
a developmental must,
you don't have any confidence
in the people you should trust.
When your innocence is taken away
and your mind's no longer pure,
it leaves you trying to understand
and leaves you insecure.
If you weren't equipped with life skills
'cause no one really cared,
when it's time to face the world
you're sorely unprepared.
You never really realized
the challenges you'd face
and you now perceive the world
as such a scary place.

## Absenteeism

Who’s responsible for what you made?
While you’re hummin’ along, the piper ain’t paid
You were just having fun and created some kids,
but you didn’t even bother

Now you’re runnin’ around shouting so loud,
“Those are *my* kids!” and acting so proud
They got your DNA ‘cause you fathered them
but you are not a father

When money was tight, you weren’t around
to offer support. You couldn’t be found
Your presence was absent
until you showed up with something in your hand

But where were you when guidance was needed,
and someone to talk to and wounds to be treated?
You came bearing gifts on special occasions
when consistency and support were in demand.

So now that it’s later, you count up the cost
of all of the moments and time that was lost.
You can’t get that time back even if you try;
no matter what you do

You can’t change a past that is acrid or bitter
so now is the time for you to consider
all of the things that can be done
to make memories that are new.

## Anything

You could have been anything,
yet you chose to be a fool
And it's not because you made the choice
not to go to school

It isn't an issue that you chose
not to go to college
But that you choose to dwell in ignorance
because you keep rejecting knowledge

Listen to what people say
when they're only trying to help
You can't figure nothin' out
'cause you keep listenin' to yourself

When offered guidance, you get mad
and get an attitude
instead of receiving what you're told
and showing gratitude

You're so defensive and unkind
that people *watch* you fall
If you don't begin to take heed,
you'll keep running into walls

Be advised that your lack of knowledge
will determine what you become
and that understanding the importance of growth
will lead to future wisdom

## Untitled

What were you thinkin'? What you don' did?
Why you keep havin' all those kids???
I know some men be fine when you peep 'em
But just because you gave 'em some
don't mean you gon' keep 'em

You always blame them; but what was your role?
Have you ever thought about birth control?
I know you wanted to be with them, but you just had to see
that poppin' out those babies wasn't no guarantee

Now you mad at all of them 'cause they won't yield to your demands
And to count yo' babies' daddies, you have to use *both* hands
Don't get an attitude with me because you think I called you out
I'm not trying to embarrass you. That's not what it's about.

It's about analyzing your options and picking the best one
And when you see the outcome, know that you're not done
We don't always make good choices; sometimes we make mistakes
But we have to change our outlook for our children's sakes

We have to be a positive example for our kids
So that they're equipped to make better choices than we did
The responsibility lies with us; we have to raise the bar
If they learn from all our battles, maybe they can win the war

# ENCOURAGEMENT

## Tidbits

Give me the tidbits and I can make a meal; tidbits of knowledge, tidbits of understanding, tidbits of wisdom. With them, I can create something to feed from for the rest of my life.

## Greater Works

When I look to the future, what I see
are the greater works inside of me.
With focus and consistency,
I will reach the place I strive to be.
It's difficult sometimes to be
assertive without apology
But determination is the key.
The bottom line "It's up to me!"
When contending with the enemy,
afflictions and adversity,
I'll stand and fight. I will not flee!
The outcome is my victory.
My challenge is that you'll strive, like me,
not to settle for mediocrity.
But to be the best person that you can be
and do greater works for all to see.

## Winning

When you're down in the dump
And all in your slump
Try to stay positive

When your relationship parts
And it's broken your heart
It hurts, but you will live

When you see the pitfalls
And fall into them all
And think that you have failed

Just keep hanging in
Because you will win
You're destined to prevail

## For Jason

To the little boy
who dreamed of mirth, comfort
and knowing what he's worth;
Look in his eyes and say to him:
*your value is worth more than gems*
Even if nobody knows,
he should; even through his woes.

To the boy
who dwelled in sorrow,
A better day will come tomorrow.
Let him know
he's loved and kept
no matter how much he wept.

To the young man
who dared to dream,
formulated a successful scheme;
who grew up from his first pities
and fought through his adversities.

To the man who reached his goals
and lived his life and gained control.
He took the wheel, steered in a race.
His drive drove him to a better place.

Keep your momentum and keep your vow.
And your success will surpass where it is now.

## Run Away

As we travel through life and experience things
Like the sadness and joy that existence brings
We will see challenges and some defeats
We will make progress and have victories
But whatever you go through, you will soon see
That you can't run away from what you must be

Life is a series of lessons to learn
Just keep on living and you'll get your turn
If you get help from others, please don't abuse it
When opportunity comes, make sure you use it
They will help you grow and you will soon see
That you can't run away from what you must be

What is your talent? Let us explore
A helper, a healer, a leader, or more?
Did God have a plan and you tried to destroy it?
It will manifest even if you avoid it
It is inevitable and you will soon see
That you can't run away from what you must be

## Your Vision

Don’t believe what they tell you. Leave them behind.
Reject what they say if it doesn’t align
with all of the things that you want to be.
Just map out your plan and they will soon see.
Don’t let the naysayers leave you in doubt.
Sometimes they won’t know what you’re talking about.
When you have a dream that God put in your mind,
you cannot expect others to find
the clarity that God showed you in your vision.
Put your faith to work and make the decision
to do what God put in your heart to do.
If He gave you the vision, He will see you through.
Be sure not to give up when obstacles come.
Just keep pushing forward ‘cause you’re not alone.
So remember your plan and stick to your mission
and all that God showed you will come to fruition

# UNCERTAINTIES OF LOVE

## The Unknown

To the man I'd like to get to know
Who's handsome, but mysterious though
We've never met. He lives afar
I don't know what his intentions are
No one knows where this will lead
This newly planted friendship seed

## Receive Accept Embrace Return

Receive, accept, embrace and return
are simple things to ask
But sometimes complications
create complicated tasks

Receive the love I have to give
My intentions are true
And even if things fall apart,
I'll still be here for you

Accept the love I have to give
Care for my heart and keep me
My warning is that when I fall in love,
I fall so very deeply

Embrace the love I have to give
I will not break your heart
Our past loves are behind us
and this is a brand new start

Return the love I have to give
Should I rely on fate?
Do you even feel the same?
Will you reciprocate?

The future holds great things to come
with everything we'll live through
Should you receive, accept, embrace and return
the love I have to give you

## Penetration

Do you really want to be with me?
That's what he always says
I've asked myself a hundred times
The answer's always "yes"

Unlike the games we play for fun
like bullseye with a dart
You've pierced me like an arrow
that's gone straight through my heart
Your full lips and infrequent smile
are pleasures to behold
You're always chill and so laid back
never brash or bold
I love your deep and gentle voice
much like an island breeze
You give me reassurance
and it puts me right at ease
You calm me and you comfort me
Your heart is very kind
And every time you hold me tight,
I know that I'll be fine
You also bring me balance.
I'm sure you didn't know
And if I get to have you,
I will never let you go

## It’s Hard

It's so hard when you want it.
It's so hard sometimes to turn away.
It's so hard that you can't look him in his eyes anymore
because you're distracted.
It's so hard to bypass.
It's so hard because he loves you
and you shudder at the thought of it.
It's so hard that you want to touch him.
It's so hard that you want it to touch you.
It's so hard because you know it will be good
and that you'll enjoy it.
It's so hard because he means so much to you.
It's so hard because he's so aroused by you.
It's so hard because he cares for you so much.
It's so hard because his Nature has risen.
It's so hard; and he's hard
And that just makes everything hard.

# HONOR

## Beautiful

Before I ever met you, it was my goal
to find someone with a beautiful soul,
who appreciates life, and all that it brings,
who relished existence of the simplest things.
You are that someone and I just want to say
that you are beautiful in every way.

## My Earthly King

Not the knight in shining armor
from a storybook
Not the one who swayed the ladies
with just one stately look
Not the one who stole their hearts
like a thief in the night
Not the one who slayed the dragon
and earned the bragging right
Not the one who feels the need
to impress anyone
Sadly enough, he doesn't realize
that he's already won
It's not a knight of whom I speak
or the fanfare that he brings
He's much more than an armored knight
To me, he is a king

## Brother Love

Strength embodied.
Power unbound.
When pride is lost,
humility is found
Subtle, quiet,
observant is he,
obtaining the wisdom.
Understanding is key.
Determination dogged.
Yet gentle as a dove.
His loyalty will always
show in his love.
Support and uphold him,
and here's what he'll do.
He'll always be honest
and faithful to you.

## Maturity

Mature with stability, that's how she comes
She's passed through the stages of naïve and dumb
Her abs ain't as tight as they were in her twenties
But her hips and breasts are supplied in plenty
She used to be the finest, but now she's just fine
You get out of pocket, she'll put you in line
Please give her the credit for which she is due
If you take care of her, she will take care of you
She's got it together, so you'd better not slack
When something goes down, she's gon' have your back
If you come at her wrong, there *will* be a fight
But she'll put that thang on you if you treat her right

## Her Majesty

Edified with majesty
Prosperity is our quest
Filled with grace and opulence
Our presence is statuesque

We are classic and unique
To disrespect us would be wrong
Our vulnerabilities may make us weak
But our determination makes us strong

Pillars of strength and dignity
Our integrity doesn't yield
Foundations in the community
And groundwork on which to build

We give the world our heart and hands
And do it for peace's sake
But when we're angry, understand
That we can make the whole world quake

We are the garden where seeds are sown
And prepared for the earth
We nourish them until they're grown
And teach them their true worth

We're irreplaceable. Here we stand
Daughters, sisters, mothers, grands
We encompass pulchritude
And perpetuate the life of man

We are majestic!

**Ode To The Black Man**

With Strength like no other, he has endured generations of pain and degradation. Although he is sometimes afraid, he takes on the world with confidence and dignity. His eyes tell the story of his life…the love, the anger, the pain; all that he has gone through. His hands show the strength of his hard work; yet they are the hands that will caress you ever so gently. His lips are full and beautiful; and always willing to plant tender kisses. He knows that his woman is his queen, but he treats her like his Ace.

He should be reveled in the highest esteem
For he is my king!

# WARNINGS

## Pied Piper

You knew he was no good for you,
But you believed the hype
He didn't have a flute and dance
His target wasn't mice

It was the women that he wooed
He knew how to entice
They were all so fascinated
By the way he laid his pipe

## Elsewhere

Elsewhere is where he goes
when you don't want him in your face
When Elsewhere, he can find his peace
and find his happy place
Elsewhere is where he goes sometimes
to have his stress relieved
Elsewhere is where he goes
when he seeks solace and reprieve
Elsewhere is the place he goes
when he ain't up under you
And Elsewhere can be dangerous
when you don't do what he wants you to
Elsewhere is the place he goes
when he's seeing what he lacks
And if Elsewhere gets too good
he just might not come back.
So be very careful with Elsewhere
if that's where he goes to play
Because he might leave home and decide Elsewhere
is where he wants to stay

# DISILLUSIONMENT

How can it be that a man will try to save you and oppress you simultaneously?

## F-R-I-(END)-S-H-I-P

After the smile, it started out flirty
And then it got real; then got really dirty.
All had gone well until that fateful night
And then came the deed, which was followed by fights
Oh, my goodness. How could this be?
Everything was fine 'til he gave me the D
Now in hindsight, I know it's too late.
I wanted that "good, good", but he gave me *great*
Now what was I to do with myself?
Downplay my feelings? Put my thoughts on a shelf?
Like a thief in the night, but he didn't steal it.
I was just another cat, and curiosity killed it.
In a moment of weakness, I let this transpire
It went from platonic to lust and desire
I wanted our friendship to turn into more.
And when I didn't get it, it turned into war
It pains me to think that things had to change
And the bond we once had would not be the same
That's how we ended up where we are now
Our friendship is over. We threw in the towel.

## bitter/sweet

Who is this man that holds my heart, builds it up and breaks it apart?

I want him to be right for me.
I want my love to stay.
I want to give him all my heart,
but something's in the way.

It's bittersweet when he is near.
I'm saddened when he's gone.
And sometimes even though he's here,
I feel so all alone.

I am Icarus; he is the sun.
I know that it will burn.
Yet I proceed. It sometimes hurts.
When will I ever learn?

Why is it that we see red flags
and sometimes fail to heed them?
We ignore them all and we proceed
as if we didn't need them.

I think that only time will show
if this is meant to be.
Amidst all of my uncertainties,
I'll have to wait and see.

## Love Kicked My Ass

The first time it happened, I was young
Infatuated with someone
But he was much older than I was
So I knew it wasn't cool

I could not wait to turn eighteen
I knew that I would be his queen
I did not know that this would mean
I'd be somebody's fool

As time went on, we did engage
By now, I was a proper age
Having him was all the rage
And all was good and fine

Then came career, and the kids
And everything I ever did
Came from my heart and was done to please him
Because this man was mine

Then crept in the enemies
In the form of insecurities
Suspicion came with jealousy
Relationship gone awry

That's when love kicked my butt
With punches to my heart and gut
Relentless jabs and uppercuts
All I could do was cry

It went from bliss to misery
It took eight years for me to see
That this was not the man for me
That's how love kicked my ass

I wanted my family intact
I stayed until panic attacked
I had changed so much and I wanted "me" back
This presence could not last

I was at a new extreme
This was not the life I dreamed
What shone so bright no longer gleamed
My joy had dimmed to gray

I found myself in somber moods
Regrouping thoughts in solitude
Trying to figure out how I'd arrived
to where I was that day

The grieving finally took its toll
And everything had lost control
Emotional freedom was my goal
I could no longer stay

I found the fortitude within
To be strong and transcend
The shackles that my heart was in
And finally walked away

## My Storm

You're like rain in my shoes
when I got somewhere to go
You're impeding my progress
I'm moving too slow
Your words are so dismal
each time that you talk
Your presence affects
the life that I walk
I was optimistic, excited and thrilled
I was convinced that my cup was half-filled
I thought you'd bring sunshine
but you brought the rain
Now I'm sloshing through life
and my comfort's constrained
Your voice is like thunder
It's scary to hear
Like lightening, you strike
inciting my fears
Where's my umbrella?
I can't go outside
The climate's severe
and I just want to hide
I long for the moments
that my days are clear
when the thunder and lightening
are no longer here
When I'm taking my shoes off
and running outside
and I don't have to worry
'cause my toes are all dry
And I'll be ok with walking alone
My stride will be upbeat
and my storm will be gone

# LOVE, DESIRE AND EVERYTHING IN BETWEEN

## Fresh Fruit

Pick me, pick me!
I am the freshest fruit!
I'm ripe and sweet
and as pleasant as morning dew
You can squeeze me, nibble me,
bite me too
And you won't be disappointed
by my juice

## Butterflies

You make my days feel so bright
And thrill me in the dark of night
I'll always love you and never fight
You make the butterflies in my belly take flight

My love for you is at its height
And you make me feel so right
I'm flying high just like a kite
You make the butterflies in my belly take flight

I love you with all my might
You support me and know my plight
You comfort me when you hug me tight
You make the butterflies in my belly take flight

## The Little Spoon

He's so big and strong.
He will conquer the world
He loves and protects
and takes care of his girl
He's hid his vulnerabilities
since he came from the womb
But all he really wants
is to be the little spoon

You're like my personal endorphin; you bring me enthusiasm, energy, and happiness.

*...my high*

## Remember?

Remember that time? I can’t forget
When I fell in love on the internet
When I met a guy and I knew he was perfect
And I’d take the risk, ‘cause I knew he was worth it
He had really nice lips and very nice arms
He was so full of life and so full of charm
He didn’t try to fill all that shit in my head
He was positive, upbeat and respectful instead
And I couldn’t wait everyday just to greet him
And I was excited by the thought I could meet him
I longed for the day I could be in his presence
He was so special. I had no hesitance
And I couldn’t wait to lay with him at night
But not to have sex; just to cuddle him tight
He was just so amazing; I will never forget
When I fell in love on the internet

## A Gentleman And A Thief

Almost perfect
Beyond belief
You're such a gentleman
And a thief

The kindest words
Flow from your thoughts
You are the one
That I have sought

Your hugs are warm
and kisses tender
You protect me
You're my defender

With serenades
Caught red-handed
You stole my heart
Just like a bandit

This is so different
And beyond belief
That I'd love a gentleman
And a thief

## His Song

I fell in love when you sang to me
Beautiful verses of pleasantries
I used to ignore the words that you'd say
But something was different about that day
You were polite and such a gent
You were sure and confident
Your presentation and your air
was oh so suave and debonair
How could you *not* catch my eye
I was flattered; a little shy
You sang of trials and your sojourn
to loneliness and then you warned
To have my love, you'd be delighted
But your love for me was unrequited
That you'd give your life and limb for me
How forever happy you would be
If you could take me as your own
So that you would not be alone
I couldn't believe what I was hearing
but it sounded so endearing
My heart was captured before long
When I fell in love with your song

I just can’t love conditionally. It’s all or nothing; and I can’t fake it.

*...as real as it gets*

## I Love You Honey

While I'm sittin' here
thinkin' about us
reflectin' and wine-sippin'
I been thinkin' about
how you be on one
and how you be trippin'
I try to keep it to myself
but I'ma speak my mind instead
I just wanna say "I love you Honey,
but I'll bust you in yo' head."

## The Man Of My Prayers

The thing about dreams
They don't always come true
But when you pray
God always comes through

Once I decided
I was ready to date
I had to trust Him
I had to wait
I had to be patient
and sit myself down
Instead of looking;
wait to be found

When I would kneel down
to say prayers at night
I prayed for God
to send me who's right
I gave it to God
and waited to see
'cause I knew He'd know
who would be right for me

Then here he came,
reserved and polite
Could this be him?
My "Mr. Right"?
At first, I was skeptical,
saw the chain of events
Now that I know him,
I am convinced

When I prayed about him,
it was hard to ignore
God's small, still voice say,
"He's what you asked for"

I prayed to God
to send someone good for me
And he sent someone
who truly adores me
He loves my eyes
He loves my lips
He loves my poetry
And he loves my hips
He loves my hair
He loves my nose
He loves my humor
And all of my rolls

He's everything and more
I could want in a man
I am willing to put
my whole heart in his hands
And I know in my heart
that he'll always be there
Not the man of my dreams
but the man of my prayers

## Alone

I cannot wait to be with you
Because alone is such a lonely place
I long to see and touch your face
I'm longing for your warm embrace

Weaving in and out of sleeplessness,
It is of you that I dream
It's really not what it seems
Because loneliness is like a scream
It pierces and its echoes sing
And always will because you're gone
But when you return,
My loneliness will be left alone

## I Call Him King

I have plenty of names
for the man that loves me
He's "Sugar" and "Honey"
because he's so sweet
Sometimes he's "Baby"
'cause he's pacified
and sometimes he's "Lover"
'cause he's by my side
Because he's my true love,
I call him "Amore"
There are so many names
for the man I adore
I love his loyalty.
He's the real thing
But because of his royalty,
I call him "King"

## His Gift

This is a story of love uncomplicated.
It's true; and it's about someone I dated.
He was quite average and not very smart,
but he gave me a gift and it came from his heart.
Expensive gifts are always a pleasure.
But they don't compare to the simplest treasures.
Will simple gifts do? Sometimes they can.
It's the most meaningful gift I've received from a man.
He looked towards the ground and lowered his head.
He gave a disclaimer, and here's what he said,
"I know this seems stupid and I feel kind of dumb.
But this gift is heartfelt and I'm not a bum.
I could have sent it with a card or a letter,
but delivering it to you in person was better.
I knew when I saw it, that I had to get it;
and it's from my heart so don't you forget it.
It wasn't pricey. In fact, it was free.
I hope each time you see it, that you'll think of me.
There are so many things that I could do for you,
but I picked *this* gift because I adore you."
He handed it to me. I began to unwrap.
I took off the paper and opened the flap.
When I laid eyes on it, I was in shock.
The gift that he gave me; it was a rock!
I was confused. Silence was heard.
I tried to gather my thoughts into words.
I had to be cautious with the words I selected,
but before I could speak, he interjected.

“Please let me speak before you start.
I gave you this rock ‘cause it’s shaped like a heart.
I know it seems odd, or even insane;
but you are my queen, and yes, you do reign
over my heart and over my mind.
You have compassion and you are most kind.
There are not enough words that have ever been written
to describe the degree to which I’ve been smitten.
So please take this rock and always remember
that I’ll always love you with every ember
that floats and that lingers and never dies down;
and will always be as intense as it is now.
To remind you of the love that I have for you,
keep it and treasure it and know that I’m true.”

A small, simple rock allowed someone to sweep me
off of my feet ‘cause he loved me so deeply.
Our relationship is over, and it’s been a while.
But when I look at that rock, it still makes me smile.
This is my story. No one would believe
that a rock was the best gift I’ve ever received.

## The One

Almost from the time we met
I have been convinced
that the fact we crossed each other's path
was not coincidence

At first, I was uncertain
But you will always be
the one I needed in my life
The one God sent to me

## Mighty

Mighty is the man I love
He cares for and he comforts me
He compliments and loves me so,
does everything to let me know
that he will long be by my side
and that his love will abide
with me until we leave this world
and that I will always be his girl.

He loves me for who I am
He's humble and he's confident.
He tells me I'm his everything;
and oh, the love songs that he sings.
I know that I will never find
another man whose heart's so kind;
and he's as gentle as a dove
Mighty is the man I love

## Beyond Forever

He said, “With every day that passes by,
my love for you grows stronger.
I won’t love you ‘til the end of time,
I’ll love you even longer.”

I replied, “Pray tell me,
You won’t leave me? Never?
Is there really such a thing
as longer than forever?
You’ll be loyal and be kind
and never go astray?”
and he replied, “You will be mine
forever plus one day.

If you need my warmth
when winter nights are cold.
I’ll hold you tight
with all my might
forever plus one day.

When I see your smile
and it lights up the room,
I’ll hold your hips
and kiss your lips
forever plus one day.

Whenever you are tired
or you're feeling down
I'll love you true
Yes, all of you
forever plus one day.

As long as I have breath in me,
I'll never go away
I vow to you that I'll be there
forever plus one day."

## Open Book

An open book as I explore,
Its cover opened on the floor.
I read through you, my opened book
with every gaze and every look.
Every scripture and every verse,
page after page, I will immerse.
Like characters in role play,
we share our love night and day.
The setting is my domain
where I am the King that reigns.
Line after line, as I read
to reach the plot and then proceed
to read a tale of my love for you.
I know your book through and through.
Just relax, release your fear
as I whisper in your ear.
I interpret as you receive
the messages that you believe
will speak to us. The scriptures read
and verses changed, which then led
to different positions and different roles.
Then I read deeper and touch your soul.
My conflict is to bring you pleasure
with every foot and every measure.
And as I read the truth and fiction,
the rhythm of my verse and diction
expresses love in its true glory,
a physical love to tell our story.

We reach our peak and then transcend
and come to a climactic end.
It almost feels like an illusion
as we reach our resolution.
As I withdraw and your book is closed.
Thoughts of indulgence in your prose
fills me, thrills me to my core.
I know that I will read some more.
Right now, I want a second look.
You are my love, my opened book.

He says that he's mesmerized by my love and charisma…
but I think it's the sex y'all.

*…between the lines*

## Some Type Of Willow

Lonely are the willow trees
that the wind blows through
Lonely is the way I feel
when I can't be with you

Like the wind through willow trees
you always come my way
But like these same elusive winds
you never seem to stay

## Her Conquest

He couldn't wait for this time to arrive
'cause he's never felt so aroused and revived
With anticipation, he wanted to know her
He had so much love and he wanted to show her
When they first met, she seemed kind of shy
He held her face and looked in her eyes
He really did love her and there was no hurry
and he would care for her, so she didn't worry
He wanted to have her; that's when he hinted
And he was surprised because she consented
He thought she was shy, but she was quite bold
She made a request that he take off his clothes
She had admiration for what she was seeing
The beautiful body of this human being
She walked over to him, put her hands on his shoulders
then kissed his lips. It made her feel bolder
Her kisses moved downward. She felt so naughty
She wanted to kiss him all over his body
He whispered her name. It put her at ease
And she was so weak that she dropped to her knees
She was so pleased with her selection
And was even more pleased with his erection
If it tasted good, she knew she'd be sprung
So she circled the tip with her lips and her tongue
Then penetration. Her mouth was full
He grabbed her hair; began to pull
Oh, she had talent; excelled at her craft
She went back and forth, up and down on his shaft

She was the best at what she was doing
He'd found a beast without even knowing
He grabbed her head and let out a gasp
Then with her mouth, she tightened her grasp
He became weak, but in his defense
it was so good and so intense
that he let out a howl in the highest-pitched voice
He couldn't help it. He had no choice
An explosion of love began to begin
and what she didn't swallow dripped down her chin
He fell to the ground onto his back
She whispered sweet nothings to help him relax
He knew in that moment that he loved her deeper
She was amazing. She was a keeper

## Strokes

My love is like an ocean
in which only you can play,
wet and wonderful
You dive to seek my treasure,
a special pearl
When you swim
your strokes are so deep inside of me
and you use every muscle within you
to reach my happy place

## Our Flight

You take me
to the moon
in a burst
of physical emotion.

We always delight
in taking this flight
and we'll do it again
night after night

## Tactile

Touch me
Tell me your demands
Touch me
with your hungry hands
Touch me
to your heart's desire
to hear the verse that you inspire
Touch me
Touch me with everything
Touch me deeply
Make me sing
My songs of love
will never leave you
as I prepare
to receive you
Touch me in your joyful play
Touch me, My Love, in every way

## Deep

His love is so deep
that it can’t be wrong
He loves me so deeply
that he incites song
Mellifluent tones
flow from my lips
When he’s deep in the ebony
between my hips

## Drowning

Like waves of the ocean
Your body continues
to return to me
Minute after minute
Hour after hour
Day after day
And every time you come
I drown in your love

## The Watering Hole

My moisture makes you grow
over and over again
Whenever you're implanted,
the succulence within
taunts you and it teases you
and rocks you to your core
And every time you take a dip,
it leaves you wanting more

## This Love

Every time you ravish me
I love you and your savagery
when I know it's for love

You knock down these walls
each time I call
each time we fuck
and when we make love

When you go down
you break me down
but you build me right back up

Like carpenters and architects
we build on this love
Ain't no façades or masquerades
We real on this love

## Collision

Like vessels, we collide in the dark of night…I love it when you're crashing into me

**Nectar**

So sweet, so sweet
The nectar in me
Delectable, so thick,
So sweet
I attract everything
Even all the bees that sting
When he looks in my eyes
And kisses me
It's so plain to see
I'm so sweet
He can't wait to put his lips on me
And his blood sugar rise
to where it shouldn't be
But he declines medicinal drips
Because he loves the sugar on his lips
He gets nectar with every kiss
And an aromatic bliss
I smell so sweet when he inhales
breathe in and in
and in and in
The sweetest scent
that he can smell
is the nectar that I give to him
It makes him smile and satisfies
It makes him happy, so happy
My nectar will always be there
And he will always get his share
For my nectar is his
and he is mine
And he can have it anytime

# LOVE’S AGONY

## The Agony Of Love

I love being in love. It’s scary though
‘cause when I’m in love, I let my *self* go
I let all my guard down and let love befall
But I feel so happy because I’m enthralled
Sometimes it hurts that I love so hard
‘cause I don’t want to give less than all of my heart
I love whole-heartedly and this is my mission:
Not to share my love under conditions
Love isn’t always what you want it to be
It’s painfully beautiful, love’s agony

## In The Mourning

In the mourning,
tears flow with happiness
that the pleasure is so great,
and at the fear of letting my *self* go.
Inside of me, you rise like the sun.
You end my nights blissfully
and make my days beautiful.
The mourning continues
as tears of joy roll down my face
because you feel so good to me.
I delight in the gratification that you bring.
Cries of pleasure and despair compete;
the pleasure of being satisfied
and knowing your commitment;
and despair at my subservience to you
and knowing that it will soon end.
But even as the tears stream down,
I look forward to always
sharing my love with you
in the mourning.

## She Wept

She wept
When she thought of the love that she had for him;
of how much she cared and how she adored him.
What she had in her heart, filled it to the rim
and whatever he asked, she'd do at his whim
She wept
The feeling she had, she could not put aside.
It was hard to explain what she felt inside.
For him, there was nothing that she wouldn't do;
and she was self-conscious 'cause everyone knew
She wept
Because the feelings she had was impossible to hide
and no one could feel what she's feeling inside.
She knew that she'd give her all to this man,
even if no one else could understand
She wept
Because her vulnerabilities were clearly exposed;
and he'd always be there is what she supposed.
Her subservience to him; it was her token
and if he wasn't there, her heart would be broken
So, she wept

## I Pretend

I pretend that everything
is how I want it to be
I pretend that I want you
as much as you want me
I pretend that everything
is perfect in our world
I pretend that I love you
and want to be your girl
I pretend that I don't think of things
that I don't want to mention
I pretend that you have all my heart
and undivided attention
I pretend when he looks at me
that I don't really care
I pretend when I make love to you
that I wish he wasn't there
I'm not sure what messages
that all my actions send
But for now, I'll just stay put
and continue to pretend

# HEARTBREAK

…and he had the audacity to ask me, "*Do you ever think of me?*", "*Do you miss me?*", "*Don't you want me back?*" Fuck no!

*…his questions*

## The Sprint

I just gathered the pieces of my heart back together
My emotions flew back and forth like a feather
When everything went south in my relationship with you
It was difficult to figure out what I should do
I was no longer full of the happiness I had
What was once joy and bliss became dreary and sad
I was so far removed from the love I was feeling
That being alone became more appealing
Though we were together, we grew apart
and what I witnessed was breaking my heart
When we first met, our hearts were racing;
so full of love. It was amazing
At some point while sprinting, we became lovers,
then tripped and fell out of love with each other
As quickly as it started, this relay had ended
and we didn't go far, but I was still winded
I was kind of exhausted, emotionally drained
And this fleeting relationship left me in pain

Being in love with reservation is not a good place to be. You get that uneasy feeling for a reason

*...heed red flags*

## The Sequel

This is now the second story
of love kicking my ass in a blaze of glory

It started out as just a fling
It wasn't to mean anything
First, we met, then started mating
Soon this fling turned into dating
He was such a perfect fit
I was certain this was "it"
My soulmate had shown up at last
and days and weeks and months had passed
It was the best time of my life
until the call came from his wife
How could I let down my guard?
I'd fallen, and I'd fallen hard
What was I to do, depart
with his roots embedded in my heart?
I'd shared my love and shared my soul
with this man. How could I dole
out so much of who I was?
I willingly did it because
I'd never felt love so profound
Within him, my heart was bound
I had to make a grave decision
I stayed, accepting my position
We continued, and planned our life
around his commitment to his wife
For me, it was a little scary
Knowing I was secondary
But I wanted us to be a "we",
So I settled for complacency

We didn't question if we'd survive
We carried on and lived our lives

Fast forward five years down the line
I was content and things were fine
I embraced our imperfect love
until it put on boxing gloves
I'd heard he had a number three
There was another *after* me
And I heard he flaunted her
How on earth could this occur?
The punches started with his lies
He hid the truth with his guise
Then came those familiar sensations
The crosses, hooks and combinations
Fight the good fight or retreat?
Or should I accept my defeat?
Should I fight for a man who was never mine?
I had already crossed too many lines
Love was kicking my ass again
I had no strength to try to win

When I began to recuperate
I had to then accept my fate
So much for complacency
I chose to bow out gracefully
Even though it broke my heart
I knew that it was time to part
Thankfully, the pain didn't last
From the last time that love kicked my ass

## Remnants Of Love

Every time I fall in love,
I'm filled with so much glee
But every time that I fall out,
it takes a piece of me
Last time I fell out of love,
it really broke me down
Mortified, I saw my heart
in pieces on the ground

Once in love whole-heartedly,
it was difficult to find
myself picking up the pieces
of my heart you left behind
My emotions had been shattered
and my heart bereft
Now I'm holding on with all my might
to the remnants that are left

# NEVER LOOK BACK

## Everything

“Anything for you”, I always said…until “anything” became *everything*!

*…never enough*

## Empty

There was a time that I likened myself
to a vessel that was to be filled
And the very act of accomplishing it
almost always left me thrilled

But even though he filled me up
there was a price to pay
I always felt so empty
Every time he went away

## Respeck

Hey, I need you to respeck me,
even though I don't
But I'm willing to sacrifice a little respeck
for something that I want

You bragged about how you get down
and how you wanted to show me
But the very next day when I saw you in public,
you act like you don't know me?

It's like you finished fucking me
and then decided to withdraw
But not just out of my body;
out of my life and all

Now you tellin' everyone
how fast I let you hit it;
and you said you cared for me.
Man, I just don't get it!

Now you ain't got time for me
So, you just dodge and duck me
Why couldn't you just close your mouth
and just respectfully fuck me?

It's all good though; when you comin' through?
I'll let you hit again
Because I'm willing to trade my self-respeck
for some dick and a little gin

## I Abstain

I abstain because God gave me strength to do it
I was lacking fulfillment and He helped me work through it
I promised myself I would stop fornicating
And I went one step further; I even stopped dating
It took God to uphold me and keep me strong
So I wouldn't continue to do what was wrong
I was aware of all my transgressions,
All my vile acts and my indiscretions

I gave away pieces of myself all the time
I left self-esteem and self-love far behind
It was quite difficult. Temptation was there;
sometimes just one guy, sometimes a pair
I'd read messages on my phone late at night
Invitations and promises of sheer delight
I would be inundated with thoughts of the act
And it took all that I had to hold myself back

After so many years, I couldn't recoup
I tried to sit down, lay low and regroup
I couldn't do it no more. What was it all for?
I look back on the days when I was a whore
It was insane. That's how I maintained;
doing godawful things that defiled and profaned
Not just one time, but again and again
But now I'm so thankful because I abstain

I fervently prayed so that I could hold fast
So that my promise to myself would last
I thank God for the growth I've attained through the years
To get where I am, it took faith, sweat and tears
I'm down to abstain for the rest of my life
or until I become somebody's wife
I'll always thank God because He's so faithful
I've learned to abstain and I am so grateful

## One Call Away

I knew in my heart there was something to gain
When I made a vow that I would abstain
To stop having sex almost sounded absurd
But I promised myself and gave God my word
With thoughts and the actions that temptation brings
Making one call could have changed everything

I was one call away from making that dash
One call away from letting him smash
I was one call away from sharing his bed
One call away from giving him head
I was one call away from other vile acts
And one call away from getting off track

If this is your goal, don't think that you can't
I know it's not easy exercising restraint
But I have to be honest and real with myself
Though I'm self-motivated, I sometimes need help
I work to stay focused and it's hard everyday
Knowing I'm still only one call away

# LETTING H.I.M. KNOW

Let the last time we saw each other be the last time we see each other

*...to my exes*

## Mr. Settlement Man

Knock, knock
Who's calling?
Who's at my door?
Mr. Settlement Man, whom I abhor

All in my face, tryin' to get another date
Last time we went out, we ate off one plate
We took the bus because you had no car
And you're saving for one in an old mason jar?

I tried to be understanding during the time that we spent
Until I found out about that settlement
You won't get a job to wait for those ends
While you ride on the coattails of all of your friends

You say you can't work, but you look pretty strong
You do everything else like there ain't nothing wrong
I can't see you no more Mr. Settlement man
Go get you a job as fast as you can!

You been waiting six years for that settlement. Wow!
You could've been stacking your own chips by now.

## Stay In Your Lane

Stay in your lane
Stop driving my life
Obligation is limited
‘cause I ain’t your wife
You wouldn’t commit
during all of our days
And although I loved you,
we had to part ways
You want to control me
and feelings still linger
But that ain’t gon’ work
with no ring on my finger
You want to take the wheel,
but you won’t get far
‘til you take the time
to invest in this star
You’re no longer my guy,
so stick to your role
and stay in your lane
’cause you can’t have control

## At Your Whim

Why do you give me the blues nigga?
Askin' me to buy you shoes nigga?
Man, I got some kids
I don't know what you did
but I won't spend my time
pleasing you at your whim

You say I don't put you first nigga
You tryin' to be up in my purse nigga?
Man, I got bills
I don't care how you feel
I won't spend my time
pleasing you at your whim

You want me with you all night nigga
If I don't, you gon' take flight nigga?
Man, I got a job
I don't care if you mob
I won't spend my time
pleasing you at your whim

You always talk like you ball nigga
But you ain't got nothing at all nigga
I got a life
Nigga, I ain't yo' wife,
And I won't spend my time
pleasing you at your whim

Why you up in my zone nigga?
While I get my hustle on nigga?
I got real shit to do
And I can’t carry you
So, I won’t spend my time
pleasing you at your whim

Now you all up in my lane nigga
Tryin’ to bring the pain nigga
Man, get the fuck out
‘cause you ain’t got no clout
And I won’t spend my time
pleasing you at your whim

## The Narcissist

So, you think I’m crazy
‘cause I speak my mind?
I can’t have opinions
‘cause I can’t seem to find
something to say
that you agree with?
‘Cause you need subservience
in someone to be with?
Man please,
I have big shoes to fill
And I cannot fill them
if I let you kill
the power and strength
that I have inside.
I will not excel
if I let you preside
over my actions
and what I should do.
I will not submit
to a narcissist like you

## Hourglass

I'm an hourglass, so don't waste my time
Running your games and droppin' those lines
I'm too old for that
So stop tryin' to jock
Just to let you know,
I've been up the street and around the block
With all that sweet talkin' you keep puttin' in my ear
tellin' me stuff that I don't want to hear
Like what you can do for me
and you'll buy me flowers
how you put it down
and can do it for hours
and the Rolex you have
and your highly-placed friends
and your "bomb-ass" apartment
and your Mercedes Benz!
If you're rollin' like that, why you braggin' so much?
Let's talk about finances, credit and such.
If you got no investments and your debt is vast
You can't get no time from this hourglass
And I checked out your rental
It was nice when I peeped it
But estate homes are "real" and you get to keep it
You got cash in your pockets; but what's in the bank?
Why yo' baby momma be lookin' all stank?
You talk about her and keep throwin' shade
But you left out the part that support is unpaid
I gave you all the time I could
You're close to getting banned
I hope you're done. Your time is up.
I just ran out of sand

## Pleasing Him

To please him:
Whatever your heart desires, Sir
Whatever you should ask
I'm here to provide your every need;
perform requested tasks

*...how it used to be*

# LISTEN WORLD

## The Problem With Tomorrow

Everyone will not have an opportunity to redeem themselves. Make peace with God *and* all of your peers. No one is promised tomorrow. Just because you expect it, doesn't mean that it will be here for you.

*...if your tomorrow never comes*

## Son Down

I can't imagine my son down in a system
designed to defeat him and suppress his freedoms
Institutionalized injustice, treatment unfair
and public defenders that don't even care.

Sometimes it don't matter what's true and what's real
The first thing they offer are plea bargain deals
To lessen the time, agreements to cop it
Our sons get railroaded and we need to stop it

Are they being fed lies or given the truth?
They serve so many years that they outgrow their youth
It happens so often and the courts just can't wait
I don't want to see my son down to their fate

If my son lost his freedom, it would cut like a knife;
or if he gets locked up for the rest of his life
I love my son and if I only make one vow
It's to fight for a change 'cause I can't let my son down

## Belong

Who said I wasn't welcomed here?
I thought that I should ask
Did you decide I have no rights?
Who gave you such a task?
I was born here. I had no choice
Yet, I'm not welcomed here?
And my ancestors who came in boats
They were not volunteers
The sentiment, sometimes unspoken
"Go back from wince you came"
Unless you're native to this land,
I could say the same
If you take time to look around
You would clearly see
That many things you want in life
Are much the same for me
Safety for my family
And safety for myself
Financial security
Wellness and good health
Tell me, are you really supreme,
or just need someone to blame?
Is your problem with individuals,
or with groups that look the same?
If I am not welcomed here
Then none of us belong
And since none of us are leaving soon
Let's all just get along

## Breathing Freely

How can I breathe
if you're holding me down?
I can't exhale.
My lungs have no sound
I'm so short of breath
and I can't get no $O_2$
I might meet my death
'cause you think I'm below you
Not an end to my life,
as in no longer living
But an end to my livelihood
'cause I'm no longer giving
in to your threats
and your intimidation
I can't just lay down
like I'm under sedation
I will rise up,
like I've been revived
I'll stay and fight
as long as I'm alive
I'll fight 'til the end
and I'll fight without pause
I'll fight arm in arm
with who's down for the cause

When you read these words,
I want you to see
That it’s not about race
or ethnicity;
(not that these things
should be forgotten)
It’s about the oppressor
and the downtrodden
If you oppress me
‘cause it gives you a rise
You might be a coward
hiding in guise
If you had some words,
you should have told me
Open your mouth
and speak of it boldly
We all have opinions
and all have our claims
But don’t disrespect
‘cause we don’t feel the same
Your disdain for me,
it never pays
and it doesn’t excuse
your nefarious ways
So please don’t give me
admonition and strife
I just want room
to breathe free in my life

## Show Your Face

Show your face.
Show your face.
Let me see your eyes.
If you won't show your face
You're a coward in disguise.
Show your face so I can see
with whom I contend.
Don't be afraid to show your face
to the people you offend.

You incite division
and have the audacity
to hide your face?
You don't have the capacity
to use better tactics
because you're a coward.
The schemes you employ
are useless and froward.
To hide your identity
is a disgrace.
So don't come to battle
if you won't show your face.

## Being Alive

The beauty of being alive is that no matter what you didn't get right the day before, you can get up the next day and try again.

*...daily progress*

## The Lives That Matter

When bullets ring out,
black lives start scattering
*Now* you say black lives matter,
but they've *always* been mattering
Look at our history. You won't get a confession
of substandard treatment and accepted oppression
It's blatantly clear, the system's unjust
Black lives *do* matter, but do they matter to us?

Our lives should matter starting at home
Our general respect for each other is gone
Are we leading our children down the wrong path?
If we don't have family, who else do we have?
Our lives need to matter within our community
For black-on-black crime, there is no impunity
One lost to prison, and one to the grave
Now two black lives lost, and no one is saved
With negative media, you know how it goes
when black women fight and get beat out their clothes
Everyone's watching; we're on the world's stage
Let's not let them see only hatred and rage

We're being watched; this should ignite us
Minus the violence, they want to be like us
They observe our look, and study our culture,
Then gobble it up like a venue of vultures
Like I said, you know how it goes
They emulate us by sagging their clothes
They're takin' notes, and taking them fast

The music, the dances, thick lips and thick ass
The best form of flattery is imitation
But give us our due; due to our indignation
Don't keep us in bondage like you want to shatter us
Give us fair treatment if you want to flatter us

Created equal? This system is strange
What we really need is a system of change
And for those who are protesting, do it in silence
Don't let our cause die, or be dimmed by the violence
It's never too late, opportunities are ample
Since we're on the world's stage, let's set an example
Let's be the great people we were meant to be
Let the lives that matter truly be free

## The Power Of Words

The power of words should never be underestimated. The words you use can have a significant impact on the people around you; significantly good *or* significantly bad. Don't allow your words to paint the wrong picture of who you are. Choose your words carefully, and with the purpose of encouraging and edifying those with whom you interact; not to tear them down.

*#powerofwords #wordsoflife*

# EMPOWERMENT

## Success

SUCCESS, I'm calling you out right now; front and center! Your presence is required.

*...elevated expectations*

## My Butterfly

I wanted a change
Things had to be different
from that day forward
As usual,
I couldn't decide
on a plan of action
So, I wrapped myself
in a cocoon
of prayer and fasting
And I emerged better,
improved,
at peace,
and more beautiful
than ever before

## Don't Count Me Out

Don't count me out because I'm female
I have other skills besides raising hell
I observe and I learn and I execute plans
I care for my kids and take care of my man
I maintain a household and keep it together
I'm savvy with finances. I'm an investor
I have a profession, respect of my peers,
and I excel at my chosen career
I serve my community, and in my church
If you're looking for loyalty, here ends your search
I'm focused and funny and so full of wit
I get down to business and don't take no shit
I've given much info, but here's one more fact
Whatever I'm faced with, I handle with tact
So don't count me out because I'm female
I'm armed with strength. I will not fail

## Stimulate Me

Here's a note to every man
who has a one-track mind;
who wants to take me out
just to intertwine

I am more than my vagina
I thought I'd let you know
I have a brain and I can think
and I'd like to take it slow

My goal is not to rack up points
or earn another notch
I'm not impressed by your willingness
to share what's in your crotch

These walls of mine are paramount;
a place of solemn surrender;
a doorway to my emotions
And only the worthy may enter

You want to stimulate my body
But I'm not so inclined
You stand a better chance in this circumstance
If you stimulate my mind

## Perfectly Flawed

I may not be the finest
but I'm still aight
The height of my beauty might be gone
and that's alright
My measurements ain't
34-24-36
It's 46DDD
and my waistline's pretty thick
And I'm missing a few teeth
Ok, maybe more than a few
But thank God it ain't the front ones
So my smile is still cool
My body got some stretch marks
and some war wounds too
But I can't change the experiences
that life has sent me through
Now let's talk about heartbreak
My heart's been beaten to the ground
And I got a little baggage
but nothing too profound
I know it's scary dealing with
the fact that I have flaws
But you can love me like I am
or don't love me at all

## Let Me Fix My Crown

I am a queen, in case you didn't know
With my royalty, comes loyalty to the people that I know
For those of you who don't know me well, let me sit you down
But before I start to give you game let me fix my crown

For the ladies who are looking for love
but settle for lust instead
Don't get upset when he only wants
to meet you in your bed
Never lower your standards
Know that you're a star
Don't hide you crown
and compromise who you really are
You take that crown
lift it to the sky
put it on your head
and hold your head up high
Understand that you've been great
since the time of your birth
and never let someone else
determine your self-worth
And when men come at you wrong,
tell their asses "Nay!"
Give them a frown, fix your crown,
then turn and walk away

This part is for the refurbished men
who want to make me your goal,
who were broken and never got fixed,
but got through quality control
You talk about my energy and tell me how you love it,
but once you get to know me, you try to strip me of it
You use your mouth and use your words
but don't acknowledge that I'm a queen
Use your eyes to recognize
my crown for what it means

I try to be the best me, as some of you might know
But for those of you who test me, here is how it goes
I'm always polite, sometimes I'm flirty
and although I'm a lady, I can get dirty
I will take off these earrings and take off this crown,
knuckle up, jack you up and beat your ass down
'cause sometimes getting attention takes more than words
Sometimes, it takes action; in spite of what you heard
But when it's all over and the dust has settled down,
I pick it back up and I put on my crown
It's ok though. You know what I mean?
At the end of the day, I'm still a queen
And one last thing before I sit down
*...let me fix my crown!*

## Vivid

I clearly see where I will be
as I embark upon my dreams,
or shall I say
the “vision” God has given me

I shall pursue with confidence
the things that I desire
while never losing sight of all
the steps that it requires

Vivid are the images
that God has shown to me
of where I’ll go, and what I’ll do,
and who I’ll come to be

## Diva

Hey Diva, you shine like the sun!
You're so full of glow
For sure, you're not done
You have people to see and places to go
Jump over barriers. Fight with the foe.
You'll be victorious in all your endeavors
And you'll have a legacy that will last forever
'cause you're a Diva
You don't have to worry
And don't you be sorry
Tell them your story
of how you succeeded
and how you'll continue to strut in your glory
'cause you're a Diva

## Child Of God

Before I was a daughter to my parents
I was a child of God
Before I was a little sister
I was a child of God
Before I was a friend
I was a child of God
Before I was a believer in Jesus Christ
I was a child of God
Before I was filled with the Holy Ghost
I was a child of God
Before I was a backslider
I was a child of God
Before I was a mother
I was a child of God
Before I was redeemed
I was a child of God
Before I am anything
I am a child of God

# STRENGTH

## My Table

Lord, where is the table that you'll prepare for me?
My enemies have arrived, and we're all waiting patiently.

*...faithfully waiting*

## To The Enemy

*Dear Enemy,*
*The attacks that you invoke on me, they really need to cease. Why you always sweatin' me? I'm just tryn' to live in peace. I just want to say, "It's unacceptable behavior." And let me tell you why it won't work; because I have a Savior. Whoever you embody or decide to incarnate, my prayers will render them useless. Their efforts, I'll abate. I'm just trying to figure out why you bother me. Just take your antics and your tricks, and kindly leave me be. I don't want to spend my time dealing with your strife. God gifted me with the Holy Ghost; so, I'm set for life! This ain't just a word I speak when I say I'm blessed. The strength of my spirit on its weakest day is better than your best. So don't you dare keep coming back, knocking on my door. Whatever you do, you'll face defeat.*
*Sincerely,*
*Conqueror*

## Legion Of Angels

I knew I had a calling and that my life had more for me
And I realized that I should let God fight my wars for me
Sometimes I faced challenges that I could not withstand
But I knew that I would be OK if I put it in His hands

Alpha marked the beginning of me being anointed
And God sent me protection with the angels he appointed
Gabriel, Michael, Raphael. They have covered me
An entire legion of angels was watching over me

Omega marked the ending of my trauma and my sadness
With my angels present, I faced each day with gladness
The journey was well worth it, even though I cried
But then, I'd think of my reward of being by His side

I know that I'm imperfect, but let me share one fact
Even though I dwelled in sin, God still had my back
I never really understood what true love could be
Until God sent a legion of angels to keep watch over me.

**Great**

Before conception, God had a plan
For every woman and every man
He had a vision; a clear view
of who I'd be and what I'd do
He would plan out my fate
He made me, and He made me great!
He made me strong and gave me strength
He gave me faith and confidence
He knew from the beginning
That He would give me other things
Like humor, wisdom, intelligence,
Understanding and resilience
He gave me gifts with so much ease
And multiple abilities:
To love, forgive and intercede
To pray for others when in need
And for some, I'm a light
of encouragement through what I write
In prayer, I can uphold them
And remind that we should trust in Him
God is loving and generous too
He also gave greatness to you

So, I'll change my statement to elaborate
God made us, and He made *us* great!

## No Weapon

When enemies come with all of their drama
And try to incite sadness and trauma
I'll be victorious and level them all
'Cause all weapons formed against me shall fall

I will not give up through all of life's threats
of perils and danger. I won't forget
that God is my keeper and His faith shall last
and all of the power that my God has

No heartache, disease, or traumatization
will consume me. I choose edification
I'll build up my spirit to where it should be
I'll have the strength to fight all enemies

I'll fight long and hard. I will not retreat
I will not concede or accept my defeat
Even when enemies come with a lie
No weapon formed shall cause my demise

The big and the small, I will reduce them
I'll lift up my hands and I will rebuke them
I was destined for greatness since the time of my birth
I know I'm saved and I know what that's worth
Some folks don't believe and don't want to hear it
I'm protected by God, and his Holy Spirit

I don't throw in no towels and don't do white flags,
'cause I know my God, and my God is bad
I'll pray and keep fighting until I ascend
Because no weapon formed against me shall win

## Damnation

What happened to us? Where did we go wrong?
When did we stop praising His name in song?
Are we here for doctrine, or just convocation?
Are we willing to bear eternal damnation?

Damnation, an anathema that should be avoided
Our lack of knowledge; enemies exploit it
They try to distract us to make us lose sight
and make us believe that what's wrong is alright

We strive to lay up our treasures on earth,
but compared to our souls, what is it worth?
Will we lay up our riches and just give Him a nod,
and not pray and worship the only true God?

By knowing His word and seeking salvation
and learning His truth, we avoid condemnation
As He looks on our lives to see what we did,
Will our offspring be cursed, or denied? God forbid

We must pray for our children for sins known and unknown
and stand in the gap, with faith like a stone
and seek comfort in knowing that we will ascend
and that all of God's promises will never bend

As He looks in that book while He sits in His chair
And tell me "well done" as I'm standing there
The threat of damnation will no longer abound
as I go through those gates and receive my crown

## This Battle

I be tossin' up prayers
and my prayers be fervent
I know God be like
"Have you considered *this* servant?"
'Cause I'm always facing trials
and always goin' through it
But God always had my back
even when I never knew it
The enemy will cause discord
with the people closest to you
He's so cunning. He will cause attacks
by people that never knew you
Trials be comin' left and right,
causing havoc to abound
But God's grace is like a boomerang
He turns those things around
The enemy be tryin' me
like I'm some kind of sample
Just like he tried Jesus Christ,
our Savior and example
But the power of my Holy Ghost
be havin' demons floored
I rebuke them in the mighty name
of Jesus Christ, our Lord
I stay prayed up to fight this fight
'cause I *will* have my crown
I'm in this battle 'til my time is up
and I'm not backing down

## Prayer 1

Sometimes it's hard to supplicate
And I can't be still and wait
When my heart's in agony
My prayer is that you'll comfort me
Sometimes when my soul is aching
and anxiety is overtaking
I know there's a necessity
to worship with consistency
It becomes a struggle just to fight
I pray Lord God, just make me light
Loose these burdens! Make them cease!
So that my mind is at peace
Strengthen me and send reprieve
Help me Lord just to believe
I need my faith recompensed
Lord God, give me confidence
Deliver me, like only you can
In Jesus' name I pray. Amen

## Back To Life

No matter how much I am tossed about emotionally, I, like a willow, will always return to my original beauty.

*...on resilience*